Make It or Bake It:
Recipes for Transitioning
Foster Youth

by
Sonya Carey

Edited by Debra Warner, Psy.D.

Artwork by Serena Hamilton, M.A.
Art Editing by Dave Warner

Published by Dr. Debra Publishing
Copyright 2021 Sonya Carey and Debra Warner, Psy.D.

Dr. Debra Publishing
ISBN 978-0-578-91960-7

Printed in the United States
1st Printing 2021

ATTENTION: ORGANIZATIONS & CORPORATIONS
Bulk quantity discounts for reselling, gifts or fundraising are
available. For more information, please contact
letslistenletslove@gmail.com

Cover Design and Illustrations: Dave Warner and Serena
Hamilton, M.A.

Dedication

To the kids who age out of the system. You are stronger than you know. You get to choose your family. Choose people who want the best for you.

Acknowledgements

I want to acknowledge the family that took a chance on a damaged kid. Four years of being in the system and eight foster homes later, you adopted me. You have supported and encouraged me and even now when I am thirty-five years-old, you continue to do so. Thank you.

Thank you to those who contributed recipes for this book.

Sonya

Foreword
Serena Hamilton, M.A.
Trauma and Crisis Therapist
Former Foster Youth

If you are reading this, I want to start by saying thank you! You may not know it, but you just became a supporter of foster children, and let me tell you, they need your support! While cookbooks often aim to inform, instruct and inspire us in the kitchen, this cookbook goes one step further. It aims to right a wrong and speak directly to foster youth who have been excluded from one of our most essential traditions: being taught how to feed ourselves.

Cooking the foods and dishes we love to create and eat permeates so much of our lives. Food is not only essential to our survival, it is cultural. It is celebration. It is comfort. Weddings, graduations, birthdays and even funerals are not complete without the right food. Family recipes are fiercely guarded and handed down from generation to generation. Grandmothers teach flour-covered grandchildren standing on tiptoes how to use their hands to measure, break eggs and follow handwritten recipes from their own grandmothers. It is the same for every culture, for every people, across the globe.

That is, unless you are one of the many children who grew up in foster care, who have come to associate food with stress, punishment, shame and loss. While there are certainly loving foster homes that strive to include their foster youth in their own family traditions, far too often, children in foster care are left out when it comes to family traditions. They are often seen as temporary guests in the homes and lives of foster family after foster family, held apart from culinary traditions and even basic instruction in cooking for themselves.

Foster children are left to watch from the sidelines, figure it out for themselves, or go hungry. It may be that they are placed with a family who excludes them out of disinterest in teaching "temporary" kids, and if your entire childhood is spent in foster care, the instruction simply never happens. It may be due to cultural gaps in cooking tradition, or it may be because of outright abuse. Many foster children report being fed very inconsistently, often only after the foster family has eaten, and hardly ever invited to participate in family meals, much less in the cooking process. Whatever the cause, the result is the same. Foster children are left to enter adulthood without basic cooking and life skills.

Enter this wonderful cookbook, aimed at addressing an often overlooked but incredibly important need for these children: Learning to cook and creating their own traditions in the absence of family. These recipes were written with foster children in mind, who may not have access to a variety of foods, tools or even basic knowledge of cooking. This cookbook sees the children that society declines to teach and forgets to include in the sacred tradition of cooking instruction and offers them a positive solution.

When I was asked to contribute to this publication, I spent a great deal of time thinking about how to best express the need for and importance of this type of cookbook to people who may not be familiar with foster care (or "the system" as alumni like myself like to refer to it) or the needs of foster youth.

I came to the conclusion that foster care survivors like myself and the amazing author of this book are best advised to use our own experiences as a means to shine a light on the issues foster youth face. My story is unique (although you may be surprised to know how common the use of padlocks is in foster homes) but likewise offers a glimpse into the stories of many others.

So many of us struggle with food anxiety, food hoarding, and eating disorders in addition to the many other non-food related repercussions of foster care that I believe it behooves us to bare our truth and seek healing.

Food and cooking in general, for me, have always been a source of stress. To be fair, it began when I was very young before foster care, when my mother started to rely on me to cook for myself and my siblings after the death of my father by suicide. And while I was not yet a foster child, the effects of neglect and trauma on my relationship with food were the same. Somedays my mother had the energy to cook and would overfeed us, overcompensating for her grief-induced neglect with food, triggering weight gain, food anxiety and later, binge eating. Other times, we were left to forage, often left to peel a raw potato and eat it with a little salt or smear some mayonnaise on a piece of bread and call it dinner.

In the absence of being taught proper nutrition and cooking, I was lost when it came time to start feeding myself as an adult, as is the case with many former foster youth and youth neglected by their parents. I started associating happiness with overeating and hunger, even mild hunger, with neglect and abandonment. It was the beginning of a self-destructive relationship with food that would last long into my adulthood.

When I entered the foster care system, several of my experiences did me no favors in this arena. Mealtime in children's home cafeterias, for example, full of sad children fed in bulk by underpaid, humorless staff, only reminded me how separate I was from my own family.

Later, it was feeling uncomfortable eating the food my foster parents would prepare, feeling guilty that strangers had to be responsible to feed me, that the presence of food now triggered guilt and shame. I began experiencing an irresistible urge to hide any food I found, take three instead of one, and enjoy it alone.

One summer, I was placed in a home that sent my food anxiety into overdrive. Besides witnessing one of the biological children stab her boyfriend with a butter knife, besides the mother allowing her children to take what they wanted from my belongings, besides the emotional abuse and having to watch the mother hit her own children, I was introduced to the concept of food as privilege. The food was served once a day, a single Louisiana hot link in a bun. The refrigerator and food cabinets were inaccessible, sealed with padlocks, the keys dangling around the necks of the biological children in the home.

They would taunt us, eating as they pleased, shoving their food in our faces, while myself, my little brother and my pregnant teenage sister went hungry. The cloudy tap water in the dirty little trailer in the desert was our only source of water. We were locked inside the trailer during the day, temperatures reaching 117 degrees inside, with no way to secure our own meals. Food would be provided when the foster mother deemed it appropriate and denied when she felt slighted in some way. Food was leverage.

My experiences, and the thousands of other stories like it, tell the truth of the sheer neglect foster youth face in regard to being taught basic life skills, coupled with trauma and other compounding factors. This cookbook speaks to that need and seeks to fill a gap that is rarely acknowledged or addressed for foster youth.

So again, I say thank you. If you are still reading this, we appreciate you. Please consider finding other ways to support foster youth in your community, as we have the nation's highest rate of children who are lost, trafficked, abused, and who end up in the criminal justice system after years of neglect and the resulting lack of life skills. We survive when we should be thriving.

If you are a current or former foster youth, we see you and we love you. Enjoy!

Table of Contents

Introduction: The Why...1

Abbreviation Table..5

    Sonya's Blend Seasoning 6

The Starter Stuff...8

    Fried Okra 10

    Pizza Fries..11

    Spinach Stuffed Mushrooms.............................12

    Fried Ravioli..14

    Lawrence's Toasted Pizza Pocket.......................15

The Hearty Stuff...16

    Turkey and Wild Rice Soup..............................18

    Beef Stew...20

    Veggie Soup 22

    Mama's Chili..24

    French Onion Soup 26

The Main Stuff 28

    Goulash 30

    All Ya Need Shepherd's Pie 32

    Lasagna 34

    Grandmadre's Chicken Pot Pie..........................36

    Big Pappa's BBQ Pulled Pork Sandwiches 37

The Meatless Stuff...38

Hash Brown Casserole...40

Mac and Cheese..42

Aloo Gobi (Potato and Cauliflower).....................44

Red Beans and Rice 46

Gnocchi with Tomato Sauce.................................47

The Sweet Stuff...49

Grandmadre's Peach Pie......................................51

Mango Chiffon Cake...52

Brownies..54

Cheesecake..55

Grandma Harriet's Peanut Butter Candy............57

About the Author..58

About the Editor...58

Introduction: The Why
Sonya Carey

Over the years my successes and failures have largely been due to me being my greatest cheerleader and my worst enemy. Despite having a strong support system in my adoptive family, I worked against myself for a long time. Being a survivor of abuse leaves an invisible mark that cannot suddenly be fixed when life settles down. This is something many foster kids are familiar with, even if they don't talk about it. Starting life with people I could not trust or rely on made me the kind of person who couldn't take advice or guidance at face value. My adoptive family tried to teach and guide me with the best of intentions, but at fifteen years old, I had become so used to the trial-and-error approach I fought against that. I have always learned best that way, even if it was not the smartest, wisest approach.

When I was almost eleven years old, I went into foster care after the death of my mother and serious physical, emotional, and sexual abuse by some of the adults in my life. Bouncing from home to home, I was able to take away a few things here and there to become the person I am today. Some of those lessons were about the kind of person I wanted to be, and some were lessons of the kind of person I didn't want to be. Foster care is different for each kid. It can be a chance to get out of an abusive situation into something better or it can be similar to the abusive environment they were taken out of. One of the consistent things about the system is its inability to prepare kids for the real world. There may be things like

1

laundry, cleaning, or personal hygiene that foster parents will try to teach the kids, but other necessary life skills are left out. This leaves many kids, especially the ones who age out of the system, ill-prepared to take care of some of their basic needs.

Even though I had people to teach me certain things, there were so many others I had to learn on my own. From filling out financial aid forms for college, paying income taxes, basic cooking skills, grocery shopping, and handling finances, a lot of things had to be learned by trying and sometimes failing. After graduating high school, I realized how ill-prepared I was for life. I could do my laundry and use a microwave and that was about it. I had a new independence that I hadn't experienced before, and I did not handle it well. I lost a job and struggled academically. Finally, a friend encouraged me to go to culinary school and learn a trade so I could make a living.

During the orientation, the speaker told us to look around at our fellow classmates. Most of these people will not graduate with you. That was scary because that had been me twice due to being ill prepared for life. Thankfully, I loved culinary school. I was passionate about it and two years later, graduated with my Associate of Science in Baking and Pastry. I decided to continue my studies and earn a Bachelor of Science in Hospitality Management. I graduated in 2016.

I am now in a master's program at the University of Southern California. At the time of this writing, I am a third of the way through and should finish at the end of 2021! The writing of this book came about as I was figuring out what to do for my final capstone project in the master's program. I wanted to do something that included foster kids. It got me thinking that there are several groups of people who are left out of conversations and have limited options in the job market. One example I found was restaurants hiring and training former prison inmates. I thought, well, why not do the same for former foster kids?

My proposal for the project will be to work with foster youth and the Department of Children and Family Services to recruit foster youth for jobs in the hospitality industry. About 23,000 youths age out of the foster system every year. A program of this type would be a way to turn around the negative life outcomes that former foster kids encounter far too often. (Vacca, 2008; Rebbe, Nurius, Ahrens, & Courtney, 2017). While in the system, these kids bounce from home-to-home gaining skills without realizing it. I know because it happened to me. I was required to adapt to change very quickly and to interact harmoniously with a variety of different people and personalities. I realized these are the same skills needed in the hospitality industry. So, I thought, "Why not put my adversity to good use!" Between that project and this book, I want foster kids to know YOU ARE WORTHY and YOU DESERVE so much more than you have been made to believe.

References

Vacca, J. S. (2008). Foster children need more help
        after they reach the age of eighteen. *Children
        and Youth Services Review, 30*(5), 485-492.

Rebbe, R., Nurius, P. S., Ahrens, K. R., & Courtney, M.
        E. (2017). Adverse childhood experiences
        among youth aging out of foster care: A latent
        class analysis. *Children and Youth Services
        Review, 74*, 108-116.

Abbreviation Table

c - cup
ct - count
ea - each
lb - pound
oz - ounces
tbsp - tablespoon
tsp – teaspoon

Sonya's Blend Seasoning

Yield: Varies
Prep time: 10 minutes

Ingredients:
(Measurement is up to you according to how much you
want to make. You can use teaspoons, tablespoons, or
cups. Ingredients are listed by ratio).
3-4 smoked paprika
3 seasoning salt or 2 kosher salt
1 coarse black pepper
2 dried oregano
2 dried basil
2 dried thyme
2 onion powder
2 garlic powder
1 ground cumin
1 cayenne or chili powder
1 seasoned pepper

Directions: Combine all ingredients well and keep in
an airtight container.

***Sonya's Tip: If you have the cabinet space, buy
large quantities of spices (16 oz bottles) from online
sources or stores. They are usually cheaper per
ounce than buying smaller bottles. Online is the
cheapest option.***

The Starter Stuff

Fried Okra

Pizza Fries

Spinach Stuffed Mushrooms

Fried Ravioli

Lawrence's Toasted Pizza Pocket

Fried Okra

Yield: 4-6 servings
Prep time: 30-45 minutes

Ingredients:
1 lb fresh or frozen okra, chopped
1 ½ c buttermilk
1 c all-purpose flour
½ c cornmeal
1-2 tsp Sonya's Blend Seasoning
3 tsp salt
Oil for frying

Directions:
1. Heat oil to 375°F.
2. Toss okra in buttermilk, coat evenly.
3. Mix flour with salt and Sonya's blend seasoning.
4. Toss okra in batches in the flour mixture, coat evenly.
5. Shake off excess and fry in batches until golden brown.

Sonya's Tip: Best to marinate in buttermilk for at least 20 minutes.

Pizza Fries

Yield: 3-4 servings
Prep time: 30-45 minutes

Ingredients:
1 bag frozen fries (Store bought or homemade, then frozen)
Oil for frying
Pasta sauce
Cheddar cheese
Mozzarella cheese
Pepperoni, small dice

Directions:
1. Heat oil to 360°F and fry the fries until golden brown and crispy (5-7 minutes).
2. Once fried, place fries on a baking sheet and top with pasta sauce, cheddar cheese, mozzarella cheese and pepperoni bits.
3. Turn on your oven's broiler and let it heat for 3-5 minutes.
4. Place the topped fries under the broiler until cheese is melted. Serve hot with dipping sauce of choice.

Sonya's Tip: Frozen fries work best. Fry the fries in batches so the oil doesn't become too cool from too many frozen fries.

Spinach Stuffed Mushrooms
Recipe contributed by Dibe Hill

Yield: 4 servings
Prep Time: 30-45 minutes

Ingredients:
4 portobello mushroom caps
2 tbsp olive oil
1 tbsp balsamic vinegar
2 cloves garlic, minced
2-3 c fresh spinach
½ c shredded parmesan cheese
2-3 tbsp heavy cream
1 c shredded mozzarella cheese
Salt and pepper to taste

Directions:
1. Preheat oven to 450°F.
2. In a small bowl, whisk together oil, vinegar, and garlic.
3. Marinate mushrooms in oil-vinegar mix for 15-20 minutes.
4. Bake for 10 minutes, stem side down.
5. Prepare filling: Combine spinach, parmesan cheese and heavy cream, season with salt and pepper.
6. Remove mushrooms, flip stem side up. Divide filling into 4 and fill each mushroom.
7. Top with mozzarella cheese.
8. Return to the oven and bake for 10 minutes or until edges have browned.

Sonya's Tip: For easy stem removal and cleaning, use wet paper towels to clean and hold mushrooms.

Fried Ravioli

Yield: 8-10 servings
Prep time: 45-60 minutes

Ingredients:
1-2 lbs of ravioli (refrigerated)
3-4 eggs, beaten
2-3 c flour
2-3 c breadcrumbs
Salt and pepper for taste
Oil for frying
Pasta sauce of your choice

Directions:
1. Heat oil to 375°F.
2. Set up a station with 3 separate dipping dishes for egg, flour and breadcrumbs.
3. Mix flour with salt and pepper for taste.
4. Dip ravioli in egg, then flour, then egg, and last into breadcrumbs. Coat evenly. Shake off excess.
5. Fry in oil until golden brown.
6. Place on paper towel-lined plate.
7. Serve with your favorite pasta sauce.

Sonya's Tip: Frozen ravioli works just as well.

Lawrence's Toasted Pizza Pocket

Yield: 1 serving
Prep time: 10-15 minutes

Ingredients:
2 slices of bread, wheat or white
2-3 pepperoni slices
1-2 tsp shredded cheese of choice
1-2 tsp tomato sauce of choice
1-2 tsp softened butter

Directions:
1. Butter slices of bread, both sides. Optional: Cut off crusts.
2. Spread sauce on one side of both slices.
3. On one side of bread, top with cheese, pepperoni slices, then a little more cheese.
4. Place the other slice of bread on top.
5. Using a fork, press sides of bread together.
6. Toast in a toaster on a low setting until golden brown or in a skillet with a little butter until golden brown.
7. Serve with extra tomato sauce for dipping.

Sonya's Tip: This is a good meal to make when funds are low. All ingredients can be purchased from a dollar store for a little more than $5 and it will last several days.

The Hearty Stuff

Turkey and Wild Rice Soup

Beef Stew

Veggie Soup

Broccoli Cheddar Soup

French Onion Soup

Turkey and Wild Rice Soup

Yield: 4-6 servings
Prep time: 1 hour 30 minutes

Ingredients:
3-4 c cooked, shredded turkey or chicken
1 c uncooked wild rice
4 tbsp butter
2-3 carrots, small dice
1 yellow or white onion, small dice
2-3 celery stalks, cleaned and diced small
3-4 garlic cloves, minced
4 tbsp all-purpose flour
4-5 c stock (chicken, turkey, or vegetable)
1 tbsp thyme, fresh or dry
1 tsp rosemary, fresh or dry
½ tbsp lemon juice
½ c milk
1 c fresh spinach
Salt and pepper to taste

Turkey and Wild Rice Soup

Directions:
1. In a stockpot or large pot, add butter and sauté carrots, onions, celery, and garlic until softened (5-7 minutes) on medium-medium high heat.
2. Add flour, cook another 2-3 minutes.
3. Add stock, rice, rosemary, and thyme. Cook covered on low heat for 30-35 minutes.
4. Add turkey, spinach, and lemon juice. Cook uncovered for another 15-20 minutes until rice is tender.
5. Stir in milk. Add salt and pepper to taste.

Sonya's Tip: Partially cook the rice to cut down overall cook time.

Beef Stew

Yield: 4-6 servings
Prep time: 2-2½ hours

Ingredients:
2-3 tbsp unsalted butter
2 lbs beef stew meat
1 lb baby gold potatoes or similar small potato
4 carrots, peeled and diced medium
1 onion, diced medium
3 cloves garlic, minced
3 c beef broth (can use vegetable broth)
2 tbsp tomato paste
1 tbsp Worcestershire sauce
1 tsp fresh or dry rosemary
1 tsp fresh or dry thyme
2-3 bay leaves
¼ c all-purpose flour
½ tbsp lemon juice

Beef Stew

Directions:
1. Season beef with salt and pepper, all sides.
2. Using butter, brown beef evenly on all sides in a skillet for 2-3 minutes.
3. In a stockpot or similar, combine beef, potatoes, carrots, onion, and garlic. Stir in tomato paste and broth.
4. Add Worcestershire sauce, thyme, rosemary, lemon juice and bay leaves. Combine well.
5. Cook on low heat, covered for 1½-2 hours.

Sonya's Tip: This recipe can be made using a crockpot. This can be turned on before you go to work and will be ready when you come home.

Veggie Soup

Yield: 4 servings
Prep time: 45 minutes-1 hour

Ingredients:
2 tbsp butter
1 small onion, diced
2-3 garlic cloves, minced
2-3 celery stalks, diced
1½ c shredded carrots
1 can whole corn kernels, drained
1 red bell pepper, diced
1 yellow or orange bell pepper, diced
1 tomato, diced
4-5 tbsp ketchup
1 tbsp rosemary
1 tbsp thyme
½ tbsp garlic powder
Seasoned pepper, salt, coarse black pepper to taste
Vegetable or chicken stock
Optional for extra spicy: ½ jalapeño, diced

Veggie Soup

Directions
1. Melt butter in a pot on medium-high heat. Add onion, garlic, celery, and bell peppers. Sauté 4-5 minutes.
2. Add stock, remaining veggies, seasonings, and taste. Adjust if needed.
3. Bring to a boil, lower heat, cook 20 minutes.

Sonya's Tip: This recipe was made using veggies that were going to expire soon. If you have produce that needs to be used up, throw it in! You can add lemon juice to enhance flavors.

Mama's Chili
Recipe contributed by Mama

Yield: 10 servings
Prep time: 3½-6½ hours

Ingredients:
16 oz red beans, soaked and drained
16 oz black beans, soaked and drained
1 lb. ground meat or meat alternative
1½ onions, chopped
2 tbsp mustard
1 tbsp onion powder
1 tbsp garlic powder
1 tbsp seasoning salt
½ c sugar or sugar substitute
1 16 oz can crushed tomatoes
3 16 oz cans tomato sauce
2 packets chili mix
3 tbsp BBQ sauce
24 oz water

Directions:
1. Place all ingredients in a crockpot and cook on high for 2 hours then turn heat to low and cook for 4 hours.
2. You can use canned beans instead of bagged beans. In this case, cook for 3 hours on low.
3. Once cooked, break up the ground meat.
4. If you want a thicker chili, use some of the juice from chili, mix with 3 tbsp of cornstarch, add mixture back into chili and cook for another 15-20 minutes.

Sonya's Tip: Large batches can be divided, put into smaller containers and frozen for 3-6 months. You will have food when money is low.

French Onion Soup

Yield: 4-6 servings
Prep time: 1 hour 30-45 minutes

Ingredients:
3 large yellow or white onions, sliced
¼-½ c unsalted butter
2 32 oz cans beef or vegetable stock
1/3 c red wine vinegar
1 tsp thyme
1 bay leaf
2 garlic cloves, minced
1 tbsp Worcestershire sauce
Salt and pepper to taste
Baguette or similar bread, sliced
3 c cheese that melts well (gruyere, mozzarella, parmesan)

Directions:
1. Melt butter in pan, add garlic and sliced onions. Sauté until brown.
2. Add stock, vinegar, thyme, bay leaf, Worcestershire sauce, salt and pepper. Taste and adjust if necessary. Boil, reduce to simmer, and cook for 1 hour.
3. Remove bay leaf and thyme (if fresh) and throw away.
4. In an oven-safe bowl, place soup with a slice of bread on top, and cover bread with the cheese. Place bowl on the top rack in broiler until cheese is melted and turns slightly golden brown.

Sonya's Tip: You can use red wine instead of vinegar for an extra hearty soup. Make sure to "burn off" the alcohol.

The Main Stuff

Goulash

All Ya Need Shepherd's Pie

Lasagna

Grandmadre's Chicken Pot Pie

BBQ Pork Sandwiches

Goulash

Yield: 4-6 portions
Prep time: 45 minutes

Ingredients:
1 tbsp unsalted butter
1 c yellow onion, small dice
3-4 cloves of garlic, minced
28-30 oz crushed tomatoes
30 oz tomato sauce
32 oz broth, beef or vegetable
8 oz water (or extra stock)
2-3 tbsp Italian seasoning
1-2 tbsp garlic powder
1-2 tbsp onion powder
3 tbsp ketchup
2 lbs ground beef (or preferred ground meat)
1lb pasta of choice (elbow, penne, bow tie)
Salt and pepper for taste
Shredded or shaved cheese for garnish (mozzarella or parmesan)

Goulash

Directions:
1. On medium-high heat, melt butter, sauté onions until slightly brown. Add garlic and cook for 1 minute.
2. Add ground beef and cook until no longer pink.
3. Drain excess fat, if necessary.
4. Add ketchup, salt and pepper, garlic and onion powder, and Italian seasoning. Mix well to combine.
5. Add crushed tomatoes, tomato sauce and combine well. Add broth mix, combine well.
6. Taste and adjust seasoning, if needed.
7. Bring to a boil, add pasta. Turn down the heat and let simmer for 20-25 minutes or until pasta is tender.
8. Serve hot with the shredded or shaved cheese on top.

Sonya's Tip: If you do not have stock or broth, you can use water and add extra seasoning.

All Ya Need Shepherd's Pie

Yield: 4-6 servings
Time: 1 hour 30 minutes

Ingredients:
2 lbs ground beef or preferred ground meat
1-1½ c carrots, small dice
1½ c yellow onion, small dice
1-2 garlic cloves, minced
1 tbsp tomato paste
1 tbsp steak sauce
1½ c beef broth
2 tbsp all-purpose flour
1 tbsp thyme, fresh or dry
Salt and pepper to taste
5-6 c mashed potatoes, fresh or instant

Mashed potatoes
1½ lbs potatoes (Yukon works best), peeled and diced
2 tbsp butter
4-5 tbsp heavy cream or milk
Salt and pepper, to taste

All Ya Need Shepherd's Pie

Directions:
1. Boil potatoes until tender in salted water (15-20 minutes).
2. Mash the potatoes with butter, milk or heavy cream, salt and pepper. Taste and adjust if necessary. Set aside.
3. Brown the ground beef and drain excess fat. Remove meat and set aside.
4. In the same pan, add carrots and onions and brown slightly. Add garlic, tomato paste, steak sauce, salt and pepper. Cook 2-3 minutes, stirring occasionally. Add meat and combine.
5. In a separate bowl, combine flour and broth, and add to the meat and vegetable mix.
6. If using an oven-safe pan like cast iron, flatten meat mixture and top with mashed potatoes. If not, transfer to an oven-safe dish and top with mashed potatoes.
7. Bake at 350°F for 1 hour. Optional: For the last 15 minutes of baking time, top pie with shredded cheese and finish baking.

Sonya's Tip: The easiest way to mash and mix everything is using a stand mixer if you have one.

Lasagna

Yield: 9-12 servings
Prep time: 1 hour 30 minutes

Ingredients:
1-2 boxes lasagna noodles, uncooked
3-4 c mozzarella cheese
1 c parmesan cheese

Tomato layer
1 tbsp unsalted butter
1 c yellow onion, small dice
3-4 cloves garlic, minced
28-30 oz crushed tomatoes
30 oz tomato sauce
2 tbsp Italian seasoning
1-2 tbsp garlic powder
1-2 tbsp onion powder
3 tbsp ketchup
2 lbs ground beef (or preferred ground meat)
Salt and pepper to taste

Cheese layer
2-3 c ricotta cheese
1-2 c mozzarella cheese
1-2 eggs

Lasagna

Directions:
1. Using butter, brown the onions and add garlic. Cook 1-2 additional minutes.
2. Brown the ground meat until no longer pink.
3. Add crushed tomatoes, tomato sauce, ketchup and all seasonings. Taste and adjust if needed. Warm all together and set aside.
4. Mix together all cheese layer items.
5. In a baking dish, layer tomatoes, then noodles, then cheese, then noodles. Continue until all product is used.
6. Layer the top with mozzarella and parmesan.
7. Cover in foil and bake at 350°F for 45 minutes-1 hour.

Sonya's Tip: To cut down baking time, partially cook the noodles before assembling the lasagna.

Grandmadre's Chicken Pot Pie
Recipe contributed by Grandmadre

Yield: 6-8 servings
Prep time: 1½-2 hours

Ingredients:
2 cooked whole chickens, shredded
5 cans of vegetable medley or mix
3 2 ct pie crusts, thawed, but cold
3 32 oz cans chicken broth
Salt, pepper, onion powder and garlic powder to taste

Directions:
1. Mix broth with seasonings and taste. Adjust if necessary.
2. Spray a large roasting pan with nonstick spray or butter it.
3. Take half of the 2 ct thawed shells and knead together to form a crust on the bottom and sides of pan. Reserve other half of shells for the top crust.
4. Mix the chicken, vegetables and broth mix and pour into the pie shell.
5. Take the remaining shell and cover the top. Pinch the shell closed around the sides. Cut a few slits into the top shell.
6. Bake at 325°F for 1-2 hours, until crust is golden brown.

Sonya's Tip: You can use fresh or frozen veggies for this dish.

Big Pappa's BBQ Pulled Pork Sandwiches
Recipe contributed by Daddyberto

Yield: 8-10 servings
Prep time: 10 hours

Ingredients:
1 bone-in pork shoulder roast, thawed
3 tbsp garlic powder
2 tbsp mustard
2-3 garlic cloves, mashed
3 tbsp onion powder
24-30 oz water (enough to almost cover the roast)
2 tbsp seasoning, salt
2 tsp black pepper
8 oz brown sugar
1 bottle (40oz) BBQ sauce of choice
Any kind of sandwich bun (French bread, hoagie)

Directions:
1. Cook in a crock pot on low overnight or for at least 9 hours.
2. Drain water, shred the pork using 2 forks and remove bone. Add brown sugar and barbecue sauce.
3. Cook an additional 30 minutes in crockpot on low to caramelize brown sugar and BBQ sauce.

Sonya's Tip: Sometimes shoulder roast is called picnic roast. Do not use boneless roast as it does not shred correctly.

The Meatless Stuff

Hash Brown Casserole

Mac and Cheese

Aloo Gobi (Potato and Cauliflower)

Red Beans and Rice

Gnocchi with Tomato Sauce

Hash Brown Casserole

Yield: 4-6 servings
Prep time: 1 hour

Ingredients:
24 oz cubed hash browns, thawed
2 c sour cream
1 can cream of chicken or mushroom soup
2 c shredded cheddar cheese (Colby Jack works)
1 tsp salt
½ tsp black pepper
1 tsp garlic powder
1 tsp onion powder
¼ c butter, melted
Topping
3-4 c crushed corn flakes or salted kettle chips
½ c butter, melted
Optional
½ c pre-cooked and chopped bacon
¼ c chopped green onions
Directions:
1. Mix sour cream, cheese, ¼ c butter, and soup.
2. Add onion and garlic powder, salt and pepper. Combine well.
3. Add thawed hash browns and combine. If using bacon, combine with mixture. (Save some bacon for garnish.)
4. Pour into a baking dish, flatten, and set aside.
5. Combine ½c of butter with the crushed cornflakes or chips.
6. Spread topping onto the hash brown mixture.
7. Bake at 350°F for 40-45 minutes.

8. Serve hot, top with more bacon and green onions, if using.

Sonya's Tip: Cubed hash browns can be found in the frozen food section at the grocery store.

Mac and Cheese

Yield: 4 servings
Prep time: 1 hour

Ingredients:
Roux
2 tbsp butter
2 tbsp all-purpose flour
1 whole yellow or white onion, fine dice
3-4 garlic cloves, minced

Mac and cheese
1 lb pasta (elbow, bow tie, penne)
4¼ c milk
¾ c mozzarella
¾ c cheddar cheese
½ c blended cheese (parmesan and asiago)

Optional topping:
½-1 c breadcrumbs
Sonya's Blend Seasoning, seasoning salt or salt and pepper to taste
1 tbsp butter, melted

Directions:
1. Partially cook the pasta in salty water. You do not want a super tender noodle just yet. Set aside.
2. Pre-heat oven to 350°F.
3. Warm the milk. Do not boil!
4. In a separate, oven-safe pan (if possible) slightly brown onion and garlic in butter on medium heat. Add flour and cook slightly for 2-3 minutes.

5. Add the warmed milk in stages, stirring each time milk is added to the roux. After all milk has been added, turn off heat and add cheeses.
6. Add salt and pepper to taste. Add pasta into sauce.
7. If oven safe pan was used, put the mac and cheese in the oven. If not, transfer to an oven safe dish and bake at 350°F for 25-30 minutes.
8. If using the topping, mix seasoning and breadcrumbs then mix with melted butter. Spread on top of the mac and cheese before baking.

Sonya's Tip: Try adding proteins and vegetables to this dish: bacon, chicken, broccoli, and spinach all work well.

Aloo Gobi (Potato and Cauliflower)

Yield: 4 servings
Prep time: 45 minutes

Ingredients:
4 potatoes, russet or similar, peeled, medium dice
2 cauliflower, small florets
2 yellow onions, medium dice
4 tomatoes, medium dice
3 tsp garlic-ginger paste
1 tsp turmeric
1-1½ tsp Sonya's Blend Seasoning
2¼ tbsp butter
Salt to taste

Directions:
1. Melt butter. Add cauliflower, cook for 2-3 minutes, then add diced potatoes.
2. Fry until tender, remove and drain on paper towel.
3. In the same pan, add onions and cook for 2-3 minutes. Add ginger-garlic paste and cook for 2-3 additional minutes.
4. Add tomatoes, cook for 2-3 minutes.
5. Add seasonings, mix well. Taste and adjust if necessary.
6. Add back potatoes and cauliflower and mix.
7. Cover and cook on medium heat for 5-7 minutes.
8. Serve with optional cilantro garnish.

Sonya's Tip: Garlic-ginger paste can be purchased pre-made. It is usually near the produce section in the grocery store.

Red Beans and Rice

Yield: 8-10 servings
Prep time: 2-8½ hours

Ingredients:
1 lb red beans, soaked and drained
3-4 celery stalks, medium dice
1 yellow onion, medium dice
1 large green bell pepper, medium dice
1 large red bell pepper, medium dice
1 large yellow bell pepper, medium dice
1-2 tbsp Sonya's Blend Seasoning
1 tsp brown sugar
4 c vegetable stock
2 c water
Long grain rice, rinsed and drained

Directions
1. Combine all ingredients in a crockpot and cook on high for 6-8 hours or until beans are tender. If using canned beans, cook for 2-3 hours on low. Taste and adjust seasoning if needed.
2. For the rice, prepare as much as you need to serve with the beans.

Sonya's Tip: Pre-cooked canned beans will significantly cut down on cooking time. You can also use a big pot and cook on the stove. If you use dry beans, be sure to soak them in water overnight before cooking.

Gnocchi with Tomato Sauce

Yield: 10-12 servings
Prep time: 1 hour 30 minutes

Ingredients:
Sauce
1 tbsp unsalted butter
1 c yellow onion, small dice
3-4 cloves of garlic, minced
16 oz crushed tomatoes
16 oz tomato sauce
1 tbsp Italian seasoning
1 tbsp garlic powder
1 tbsp onion powder
1½ tbsp ketchup

Gnocchi
4 potatoes
3 c flour
2 eggs
Salt and pepper to taste

Directions:
1. Poke holes into potatoes and bake at 400°F until tender (45 minutes-1 hour).
2. Cut in half and scoop out the insides. Mash in a large bowl.
3. Stir in flour, salt, pepper, egg, and any other ingredients you are using.
4. Mix well until a dough forms.
5. On a lightly floured surface, divide dough into even pieces.

6. Roll out each piece into a long rope and cut each rope into even pieces about ½ inch long.
7. Bring a pot of salted water to a boil and add the gnocchi in batches. Boil until tender (4-5 minutes), transfer to a bowl or directly into the tomato sauce.

Sonya's Tip: You can play around with gnocchi by adding other flavors into the dough. Options include minced spinach, minced basil, parmesan cheese, and minced tomatoes.

The Sweet Stuff

Grandmadre's Peach Pie

Mango Chiffon Cake

Brownies

Cheesecake

Grandma Harriet's Peanut Butter Candy (Fudge)

Grandmadre's Peach Pie
Recipe contributed by Grandmadre

Yield: 6-8 servings
Prep time: 1½-2 hours

Ingredients:
3 2 ct deep dish pie crusts, thawed but cold
3 15¼ oz cans of peaches
½ lb salted butter, cubed
3-4 tsp nutmeg
3 c sugar
1 tbsp vanilla extract
1-2 tsp cornstarch for thicker filling

Directions:
1. Take half of the thawed shells and knead together to form a crust on the bottom and sides of the pie dish. Reserve remaining half for the top crust.
2. Mix peach, nutmeg and vanilla and spoon half of mixture into the shell. Place half the butter on top of the mixture. Repeat process until all ingredients are used.
3. Cover the pie with the remaining crust cut in strips so it forms a lattice.
4. Bake at 325°F for 1-1½ hours until crust is golden brown.

Sonya's Tip: ClearJel is an alternative to cornstarch and is more effective. You do not have to use as much. Pricewise there is not a huge difference.

Mango Chiffon Cake

Yield: 10-12 servings
Prep time: 1 hour-1 hour 30 minutes

Ingredients:
Cake
2 c all-purpose flour, sifted
2½ c sugar or sugar substitute
1 tbsp baking powder
½ tsp cream of tartar
1 tsp salt
7 egg yolks
7 egg whites
¾ c water
¾ c mango puree
1 tsp lemon juice
½ c vegetable oil
1 c mango, ripe and diced

Frosting
2 c unsalted butter, soft
½ c heavy cream
6 c powdered sugar
½ c mango puree
1 tsp lemon juice

Directions
1. Pre-heat oven to 350°F.
2. Sift together flour, ¾ c sugar, salt and baking powder.

3. Beat egg whites with cream of tartar. When almost at stiff peaks, add remaining sugar (¾ c), beat and set aside.
4. In a separate bowl, combine dry ingredients with oil, yolks, lemon juice and mango puree and mix well.
5. Using a spatula, fold egg whites into the other mixture in batches.
6. Pour batter into greased pan and bake for 45 minutes. Cool completely.
7. For icing, cream butter and 1 c powdered sugar.
8. Add remaining powdered sugar and heavy cream, alternating until used.
9. Add lemon juice and puree. Refrigerate until ready to use. Frost cake after it has cooled and garnish with fresh, ripe mangos, if desired.

Sonya's Tip: Try this recipe with other fruit like strawberries.

Brownies

Yield: 8-10 servings
Prep time: 40 minutes

Ingredients:
1-1½ c chocolate chips
¾ c butter
1¼ c sugar or sugar substitute
3 eggs
2 tsp vanilla extract
¾ c all-purpose flour
¼ c cocoa powder
1 chocolate pudding cup
1 tsp salt

Directions:
1. Preheat oven to 350°F.
2. Chop chocolate and melt in microwave-safe bowl, stirring at 20-30 second intervals.
3. Mix butter with sugar Add eggs, vanilla, and pudding.
4. Whisk in melted chocolate.
5. Mix in flour and cocoa powder and combine thoroughly.
6. Pour into a greased pan.
7. Bake for 25 minutes.

Sonya's Tip: Experiment with different flavors of chocolate and caramel.

Cheesecake

Yield: 8-10 servings
Prep time: 4 hours-overnight

Ingredients:
Filling
3 lbs cream cheese
1¾ c sugar
1 lemon for juice and zest
1 tsp vanilla extract
5-6 eggs
4 oz butter

Crust
Crushed graham crackers
3-4 oz butter, melted

Directions:
1. Cream butter and cream cheese.
2. Zest the lemon, then cut and squeeze juice into a separate bowl.
3. Add zest, juice, vanilla, and sugar to the cream cheese, combine well.
4. Add eggs one at a time, beating after each egg. Combine well until a batter a little thicker than cake batter forms.
5. Mix crushed graham crackers with the butter so it holds together like wet sand.
6. Grease cake pan and form the crust by pressing graham cracker mixture to bottom and sides. Pour in batter.

7. Place cake pan in a bigger pan or baking dish and fill larger pan with water to about halfway.
8. Bake at 375°F until top of cheesecake is golden brown (1-1½ hours). Cool completely overnight in the refrigerator before eating.

Sonya's Tip: Let the cheesecake cool at room temperature for 2-3 hours before refrigerating. You can also use sandwich cream cookies as a crust but use less butter. Top with fruit, candy pieces or cookie pieces, as desired.

Grandma Harriet's Peanut Butter Candy
(Fudge)
Recipe contributed by Daddyberto
Yield: 12 servings
Prep time: 1 hour

Ingredients:
2 c sugar
½ c milk
2 heaping tbsp peanut butter

Directions:
1. In a saucepan, add sugar and milk and bring to a boil.
2. Reduce heat to low and simmer for 7 minutes or until sugar dissolves, stirring constantly.
3. Take off heat and stir in peanut butter.
4. Lightly butter a pan and pour in mixture. Let set.

Sonya's Tip: This recipe can be made with other types of nut butters or peanut butter substitutes like sunflower butter. However, it does not work well with sugar substitutes.

About the Author

Sonya Carey
Sonya Carey was a former foster youth who moved several times in a four-year period before being adopted by one of her foster families. At the age of twenty-seven, she went back to college to pursue a degree in Baking and Pastry (A.S) and Hospitality Food and Beverage Management (B.S.). She is currently pursuing a master's degree in Hospitality and Tourism at the University of Southern California. Most recently, she worked as a Food Service Manager, overseeing several food service locations. She has more than fifteen years of experience in the food service industry.

About the Editor

Debra Warner, Psy.D.
Dr. Debra, Mama
Dr. Debra is a leading forensic psychologist, popular speaker, trauma expert, training professional and author, as well as Sonya Carey's proud Mama! She never thought she would share her passion for cooking with her daughter, who would then share it with the world. For all displaced children in the system, never give up your dream. YOU CAN DO IT!

NOTES

_____

_____

_____

_____

_____

_____

_____

_____

_____

_____

_____

_____

_____

_____

_____

_____

_____

_____

_____

_____

_____

_____

_____

_____

_____

_____

_____

_____

_____

_____

_____

_____

_____
_____
_____
_____
_____
_____
_____
_____
_____
_____
_____
_____
_____
_____
_____
_____
_____
_____
_____
_____
_____
_____
_____
_____
_____
_____
_____
_____

_____
_____
_____
_____
_____
_____
_____
_____
_____
_____
_____
_____
_____
_____
_____
_____
_____
_____
_____
_____
_____
_____
_____
_____
_____
_____
_____
_____
_____
_____
_____

CPSIA information can be obtained
at www.ICGtesting.com
Printed in the USA
BVHW020303270721
612868BV00020B/1264